Sharks

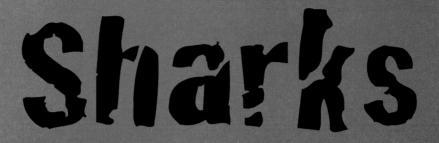

Jonathan Sheikh-Miller

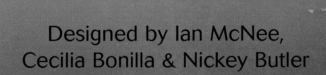

Designed by Ian McNee,
Cecilia Bonilla & Nickey Butler

Illustrated by John Woodcock
Consultants: Theresa Greenaway
& Dr. Frances Dipper

Contents

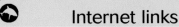

Internet links

For links to the websites recommended in this book, go to the Usborne Quicklinks Website at **www.usborne-quicklinks.com** and enter the keyword "sharks". Usborne Publishing is not responsible for the content on any website other than its own. Please read the Internet safety guidelines on the Usborne Quicklinks Website and on page 62 of this book.

★ Pictures in this book with a star symbol beside them can be downloaded for your own personal use from the Usborne Quicklinks Website.

Left: Grey reef sharks swimming at Bikini Atoll in the Pacific Ocean

A grey reef shark feeding in the Pacific Ocean

What is a shark?

A shark is a type of fish and there are about four hundred different kinds, or species, of sharks. Most sharks live in the sea, although a few species are found in rivers too.

This group of small fish is staying close to a huge whale shark for protection.

Size matters

Sharks have the reputation of being huge, ferocious killers. But fewer than a fifth of them are bigger than humans. On average, a shark is only about 60-90cm (2-3ft) long. The biggest shark, the whale shark, is longer than a bus, while one of the smallest, the spined pygmy shark, is about the size of a banana.

Taking shape

Many sharks are grey, with long, torpedo-shaped bodies. But there are lots of sharks with very different shapes. For example, hammerheads have distinctive, flattened heads, and a number of sharks that live on the seabed have flat bodies.

A flat-bodied angel shark

A scalloped hammerhead shark

Are sharks dangerous?

Although about thirty species of sharks have attacked humans, only a few are thought to have killed them. Shark attacks are rare and most don't cause serious injury. Sharks such as the basking shark are big enough to hurt or kill humans, but are harmless.

Internet links

For links to websites where you can watch divers swim with sharks, view video clips of unusual sharks and see where sharks live, go to **www.usborne-quicklinks.com**

Basking sharks are big, but harmless.

Where do sharks live?

Sharks live in all different parts of the world, from warm tropical seas to cold polar waters. Some live deep down at the bottom of the sea, while others always swim near the surface.

Many sharks live on coral reefs. These rock-like structures are found in warm, shallow, clear water and are made of the skeletons of tiny animals called coral polyps.

This is a coral reef in the Red Sea.

Not like other fish

Most fish, like people, have skeletons made from bone. But all sharks have skeletons made of a lightweight, flexible material called cartilage.

Shark parts

Although different types of sharks can look very different from one another, they also have many important characteristics in common.

A typical shark

The sharks in the main picture are what most people think of as typical sharks. They have streamlined bodies, which means that their shape allows them to slip easily through the water.

Here are two Caribbean reef sharks swimming side by side. The labels indicate some of the features common to most sharks.

Many sharks have long pointed snouts, which help them to swim smoothly through the water.

These openings are called gill slits. Inside them are the shark's gills, which it uses for breathing.

Shark skin

A shark's skin is covered in tiny, thorn-like hooks called denticles, which feel rough to the touch. These help to protect the shark from injury.

A close-up view of denticles on a shark's skin

This is one of a pair of pelvic fins. These fins are a little like the back legs or limbs of other animals.

This triangular fin is called a dorsal fin. Sharks have one or two of these on their backs.

Internet links

For links to websites packed with fascinating shark facts, pictures and a slide show of different sharks, go to **www.usborne-quicklinks.com**

Upper lobe

This is a pectoral fin. All sharks have two of these, one on each side of their bodies. They are similar to the front legs or limbs of other animals.

Lower lobe

A shark's tail consists of two sections called the upper and lower lobes.

Fin features

A shark's fins are among its most important features. Where many animals have a pair of front and back legs, sharks have a pair of pectoral and pelvic fins. Fins help sharks to balance and change direction in the water.

Sharks are best-known for the dorsal fin, or fins, on their backs, which can sometimes be seen poking above the sea's surface.

A shark's triangular dorsal fin poking above the surface is instantly recognizable.

★

How sharks swim

Some sharks are faster swimmers than others, but they all move through the water in the same way. All sharks need to be able to swim to look for food and also to escape from any other animals that might decide to attack them.

Power sharks

This shows the equal-sized lobes of a mako's tail. These give it a curved, crescent moon shape.

The sharks that are the most powerful swimmers have large crescent-shaped tails that can produce a big forward thrust.

This oceanic whitetip is swimming quickly near the sea's surface.

Internet links

For links to websites where you can watch video clips of sharks, find out more about how fish swim and try a shark quiz, go to **www.usborne-quicklinks.com**

Swimming style

Sharks swim by beating their tails from side to side. As the tail swings, it pushes against the water. The force that this produces gives the shark's body a strong forward thrust.

Some sharks look like the letter 'S' as they swim because their bodies move from side to side.

The shark swings its tail from side to side to push itself through the water.

Fantastic fins

A shark's pectoral and pelvic fins look and act a little like aircraft wings. As water flows over the fins, lift is created which stops the shark from sinking. To rise up, a shark tilts its pectoral fins slightly.

The shark is tilting its pectoral fins slightly to get extra lift.

This blue shark is rising up to the surface.

Turning and stopping

★ This picture shows a flexible starry smooth-hound shark making a quick u-turn.

To turn around, some sharks can bend their bodies into a horseshoe shape so that they can completely change direction. Less flexible sharks tilt their pectoral fins and curve their bodies slightly to make a more gradual turn.

To slow down, sharks angle their pectoral fins and push against the water, so the fins act like brakes.

Scrambling sharks

Some sharks that spend a lot of time on the seabed sometimes prefer not to swim. Instead, they use their pectoral fins to scramble along.

This nurse shark is using its pectoral fins to clamber along the seabed.

Basic shark senses

Sharks have well-developed senses which are suited to their underwater world. They use these to avoid predators (animals that hunt other animals) and to hunt for prey (other animals to eat).

A protective layer of skin is partly covering the eye of this oceanic whitetip shark.

View to a kill

When sharks attack their prey, they can get injured. Some sharks, such as the oceanic whitetip, have layers of skin that cover and protect their eyes.

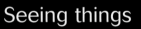

Seeing things

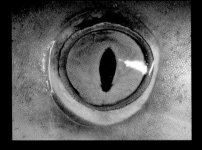

At night, the reflective layer at the back of a shark's eye makes it shine brightly.

Sharks have good eyesight. In deep, dark water, they use a reflective layer at the back of their eyes to help them see. This acts a little like a mirror and makes better use of the dim light that enters their eyes.

Blind attack

Sharks that don't have a protective layer of skin roll their eyes back into their heads when they attack. This means they can't actually see their prey as they prepare to bite it.

Hearing sounds

Sharks' ears are inside their heads. They have two ears, one on either side of the brain. They are good at hearing deep, low-pitched sounds.

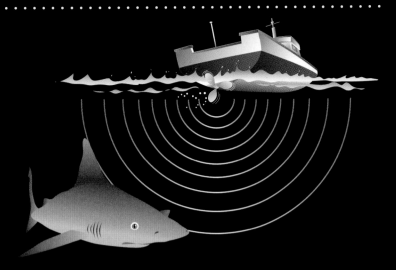

A shark can easily hear the low noise of a boat's motor from some distance away.

On the scent

Sharks have two nostrils on their snouts. They don't use these for breathing, but for smell. As sharks swim, water passes into their nostrils and then over a special layer of skin that can detect smells.

The large nostrils on this Caribbean reef shark's snout help it to sniff out fish to eat.

Good and bad taste

Sharks have taste cells, or buds, spread over small bumps on the roofs of their mouths and on their tongues. These enable them to taste their food and decide if they want to eat it or not. Despite this, they do sometimes eat junk such as tin cans, plastic bags and bottles.

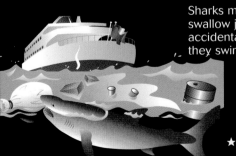

Sharks may swallow junk accidentally as they swim along.

Fact: Sharks have an excellent sense of smell and can detect blood nearly two miles away.

Special senses

Sharks have some unusual senses that make them good hunters. They can feel the movements of other animals nearby and can even sense electric signals given off by them.

Electric detectives

All animals give off electric signals through their muscles and nerves. Sharks can detect these signals through small holes, or pores, on their snouts. This helps them locate prey.

The black dots on the snout of this sand tiger shark (also called the grey nurse shark) are pores that can detect electric signals.

Metal munchers

Sometimes sharks attack metal objects. In salty sea water, metals give off weak electric signals which confuse sharks. They may mistake metal objects for their prey and then launch an attack.

This great white is attracted by the electric signals given off by the diver and his protective metal cage.

Feeling for food

Sharks can "feel" the presence of a
predator or prey, without having to see it.
Under their skin, they have tubes containing
tiny hairs which can detect the slightest
movement in the water around them.

 Internet links

For links to websites where you can
explore a clickable picture of a shark,
discover more about shark senses and
find tips on drawing sharks, go to
www.usborne-quicklinks.com

The red line shows the area on
a shark's body that can "feel" a
nearby animal. The area is the
same on both sides.

Hidden delights

Some sharks that live on the seabed rely
on their sense of touch to find food. They
have stubs or strips of skin, called barbels,
on the end of their snouts. They use these
to feel for any prey that might be hiding
under the sand.

Feel and taste

Barbels are covered with small
taste buds, so that sharks can
taste their prey while they are
feeling it, to test whether
it's good to eat.

This epaulette shark has
short barbels on the end
of its snout.

Gills and breathing

All animals need oxygen to live. Many get it from the air using their lungs. But sharks and other fish use their gills to take oxygen from the water around them.

Breathing on the move

Very active sharks that spend most of their time swimming breathe by keeping their mouths and gill slits open. Water can then flow freely over their gills. A shark's gills contain tiny tubes called blood vessels. These absorb oxygen from water as it passes over them.

Great whites are very active sharks and use up a large supply of oxygen.

Open and shut

Sharks that are not always on the move mostly use another method of breathing. To start with, a shark opens its mouth and takes in water, but keeps its gill slits closed. It then closes its mouth and opens its gill slits so that the water is pushed out over the gills.

This reef shark has opened its mouth to let in water.

When it closes its mouth, the water goes out through its gill slits.

Fact: Water contains much less oxygen than air does, so sharks need a large, continuous flow of water in order to breathe in enough oxygen.

Spiracle users

Sharks that spend a lot of their time resting on the seabed have an alternative way of breathing. They have holes called spiracles, just behind their eyes, which they can use to suck in water. This means they can breathe even if they are buried under sand on the seabed, because they don't need to open their mouths.

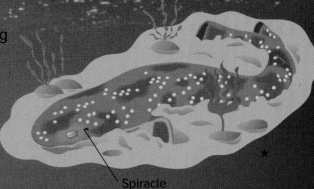

Spiracle

This shows a Gulf catshark on the seabed using its spiracle to breathe.

 ### Internet links

For links to websites where you can find out more about how fish breathe and see if you're a shark expert with an online quiz game, go to **www.usborne-quicklinks.com**

Sleeping reef sharks

Even some active sharks take breaks on the seabed. Caribbean reef sharks are sometimes found resting on the ocean floor. When they do this, they don't use their spiracles but just breathe normally, by sucking water into their mouths.

Caribbean reef sharks take breaks on the seabed during the day.

Teeth and eating......................

Many sharks have ferocious-looking teeth. But others have flat teeth, and some have tiny teeth that are not used at all for eating. The shape of a shark's teeth is suited to the kind of food it eats.

A great white's teeth are about 7cm (3in) long and can easily tear through the flesh of large prey.

Triangular terrors

Big sharks like the great white, tiger shark and blue shark have triangular teeth with jagged edges. These are good for catching hold of large fish and animals, and tearing chunks of meat from them.

Fish hooks

Sand tiger sharks have long, narrow teeth which make them look very fierce. These are ideal for grabbing hold of slippery prey, like fish and squid, that are often eaten whole.

A sand tiger shark's pointed teeth may make it look frightening, but in fact this shark is not very aggressive.

Fact: During its lifetime, a shark will grow, and then lose, thousands of teeth.

Endless teeth

Sharks that hunt need strong, efficient teeth for killing and eating their prey. Sharks have several rows of teeth. When a front tooth breaks or wears down, one from behind moves forward to fill the gap.

Shell crushers

Not all sharks have sharp teeth. Horn sharks have pointed front teeth, but flat, blunt back teeth. They feed on small animals covered by tough shells, such as sea-urchins. The flat teeth can crush through the shells.

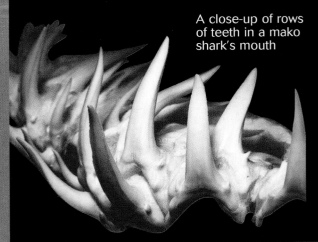

A close-up of rows of teeth in a mako shark's mouth

Pointed teeth at the front of a horn shark's mouth

Flat teeth

Tiny teeth

Some of the biggest sharks, like the whale shark and the basking shark, have very small teeth. They don't actually need to use their teeth for biting, as they have a different way of eating from other sharks (see page 28).

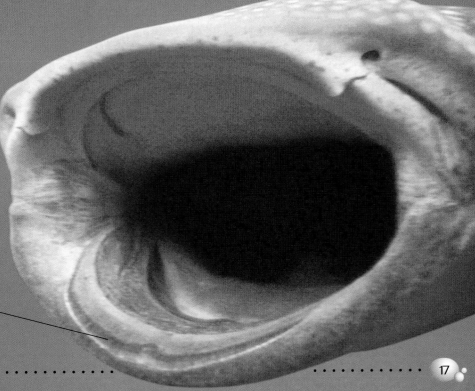

If you look hard, you can just see a row of tiny teeth here.

Going in for the kill

Sharks have different ways of attacking their prey. Most sharks work alone, but some hunt in groups. They are usually calm hunters, but can become frenzied killers.

One-bite hunter

The great white attacks its prey by biting it just once. It then moves off a short distance to wait for the victim to weaken or die, before returning to eat it. It does this to avoid injury in a struggle.

Big biters

Some big hunters have very powerful bites. This is because their jaws are only loosely connected to their skulls, so they can open their mouths very wide.

★

When a shark opens its mouth to bite its prey, its head and snout rise up and its jaws begin to move apart.

When the jaws are fully open, the upper jaw and teeth move forward, allowing the shark to take a powerful bite.

This great white is about to deliver a massive bite to its next victim.

Group killers

Some sharks hunt in groups. For example, blacktip reef sharks work together to round fish up. They then drive them into shallow water and onto the beach. The sharks wriggle onto the beach, snatch the fish and then swim off.

This shows blacktip reef sharks chasing fish onto a beach.

Feeding frenzies

When a group of sharks find a large number of fish, they can become very agitated. They madly attack the fish and sometimes they bite each other in their excitement. This is called a feeding frenzy.

These grey reef sharks have found a large supply of food and may soon go into a feeding frenzy.

 Internet links

For links to websites with an animation of the deadly jaws of the great white shark and pictures of sharks jumping out of the water as they hunt, go to **www.usborne-quicklinks.com**

Pup producers

Many animals, such as birds, lay eggs and babies hatch out from them. Some sharks do this too. But the babies of most sharks stay inside their mothers until they are fully developed. The mother then gives birth to baby sharks, which are called pups.

Getting together

To produce babies, sharks have to find a mate, or partner of the opposite sex. Female sharks attract the attention of males by releasing perfumed chemicals into the water. If a male shark is interested, it may chase after the female and bite it.

This male whitetip reef shark is biting a female shark to show that he is interested in her.

Making babies

A baby shark starts to form when a sperm cell from a male shark joins together with an egg inside a female shark. Before this can happen, a male shark has to push sperm into a female's body using a part of its body called a clasper. The sperm enters the female's body through a hole called a cloaca. This is called mating.

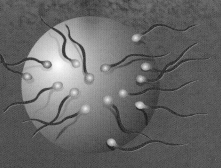

Millions of sperm enter a female's body but only one can join together with the egg to start forming a baby shark. Here, the pink shapes are sperm and the blue sphere is the egg.

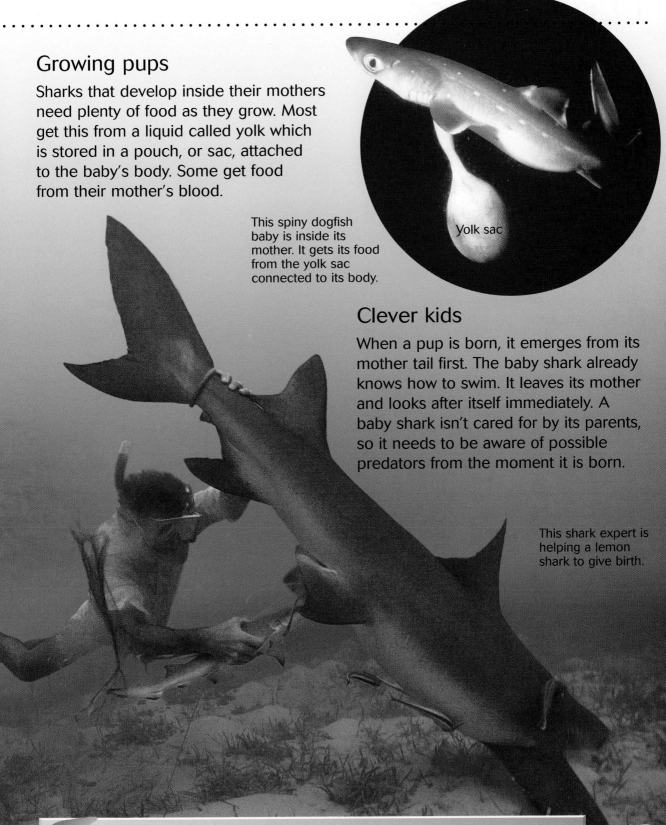

Growing pups

Sharks that develop inside their mothers need plenty of food as they grow. Most get this from a liquid called yolk which is stored in a pouch, or sac, attached to the baby's body. Some get food from their mother's blood.

Yolk sac

This spiny dogfish baby is inside its mother. It gets its food from the yolk sac connected to its body.

Clever kids

When a pup is born, it emerges from its mother tail first. The baby shark already knows how to swim. It leaves its mother and looks after itself immediately. A baby shark isn't cared for by its parents, so it needs to be aware of possible predators from the moment it is born.

This shark expert is helping a lemon shark to give birth.

Fact: While they are still inside their mothers, baby sand tiger sharks may eat their own brothers and sisters to get strong and healthy.

Laying eggs.............

Some species of sharks lay eggs. The baby shark grows inside the egg and emerges when it is fully developed.

Staying alive

While it is inside its egg, a baby shark gets its food from the yolk sac attached to it. Water can also enter the egg case so that the baby shark can breathe in plenty of oxygen from it.

Shark eggs

Shark eggs come in different shapes and sizes. A lot are shaped like purses or pouches, and all have strong cases to protect the baby inside. Some eggs have long cords on them. When the mother lays an egg, the cords get tangled around objects on the seabed and this stops the egg from floating away.

It is easy to see the baby draughtsboard shark and its large yolk sac inside this egg case.

This egg case has long cords on it which will wrap around plants on the seabed to anchor it in place.

Egg twisters

Horn shark eggs don't have any cords on them, but do have strange-looking twisted cases. To protect them, female horn sharks often carry the newly laid eggs in their mouths and place them in small rock crevices.

This horn shark egg has been left on top of a rock, and not in a crevice.

Eggs at risk

Sharks do not guard their eggs, so baby sharks are open to many dangers. Some are eaten by predators, while stormy weather at sea can also push eggs out from their resting places. Many are washed up on beaches, where the eggs dry out and the babies inside them die.

This Australian swellshark egg has been washed up on a beach.

Hatching out

Some sharks spend longer in their eggs than others. But once they have used up all the yolk, it is time to break out of the egg, or hatch, and start looking for food.

Mothers lay their eggs where there is a good supply of food to be found by the young sharks.

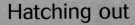

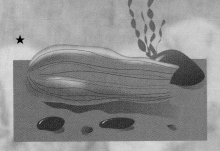

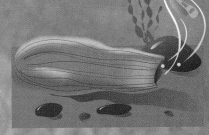

The swellshark inside this egg case is ready to hatch.

To tear the case apart, the shark pushes against the end.

The tiny shark is able to swim away immediately.

This swellshark is just breaking out from its egg case and is about to swim away.

Great white

The great white is the best-known type of shark. It is also known as the "white death" because of its reputation as a man-eater.

Frightening whites

Great whites are the largest meat-eating shark, growing to around 6m (18ft) long. They have sharp, strong teeth and a very powerful bite.

Here you can see the size of a great white compared with a diver.

Hungry for humans?

Although great whites are dangerous and do sometimes kill people, human flesh is not their normal food. They much prefer seals because their fatty flesh provides a lot of energy.

This northern elephant seal would provide a good meal for a great white.

Surface sharks

Great whites usually attack at the sea's surface. They swim up to their target from below, sometimes thrusting their heads and part of their bodies right out of the water as they attack.

Great whites can suddenly appear above the surface, looking around for their next meal.

Fact: After a large meal, a great white may not eat again for many weeks.

This great white is swimming close to the surface, looking around for its next meal.

Watching out for whites

Great whites live in cool coastal waters in places like Australia, South Africa, the U.S.A. and the Mediterranean. They are not an especially common type of shark and in some areas they are now a protected species.

Great whites are only rarely seen, so meeting one would be very unusual.

 Internet links

For links to websites where you can watch videos of great white sharks, browse a photo gallery and play a survival game where you are a hungry tiger shark, go to **www.usborne-quicklinks.com**

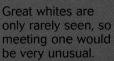

Dangerous sharks

Tiger, bull and oceanic whitetip sharks are all very dangerous and can easily kill large prey. Luckily, the chances of a person being attacked by a shark are very small.

Great white tigers

Young tiger sharks have a striped pattern a little like that of a tiger. But, as they get older, their stripes fade and they begin to look like another big hunter – the great white.

This tiger shark is hungrily biting the flesh of a dead whale.

Easy pickings

Tiger sharks often eat baby albatrosses. Each year, they gather near the Hawaiian islands, where large numbers of these birds live. They wait for the young birds to fall into the sea as they learn how to fly, and then snap them up..

A young albatross makes an easy target.

Fact: The largest and most powerful sharks will attack and eat all kinds of prey, including squid, dolphins and even other sharks.

The open ocean killer

Oceanic whitetips spend most of their time far out at sea, so they don't present much of a threat to people.

However, it is thought that oceanic whitetips have attacked and killed people who have ended up in the sea after shipwrecks or plane crashes.

An oceanic whitetip

Bull sharks

Most sharks can only live in salty sea water, but bull sharks sometimes swim up rivers. They have been seen in the Amazon river in Peru around 4,000 km (2,500 miles) from where it joins the sea.

This bull shark is swimming slowly, waiting for its next victim to come too close.

Dangerous rivers

Bull sharks are only about 3m (10ft) long, but they have been known to attack large animals such as hippopotamuses and even people. Stingrays, which are related to sharks, also sometimes badly injure people wading in tropical rivers.

Plankton eaters

Some of the biggest sharks feed on the smallest living things in the sea. Tiny animals and plants, called plankton, are a main source of food for three huge sharks: the whale shark, basking shark and megamouth.

What is plankton?

Plankton is the name used to describe tiny plants and animals that float near the sea's surface. Some are so small that they can only be seen through a microscope.

Plankton

The biggest fish

The whale shark is the world's largest fish. It is about eight times as long as an average person, and each of its pectoral fins is 2m (6ft) long.

A whale shark sucks in water like a giant vacuum cleaner and filters food out from it. In an hour, it can suck in hundreds of bucketfuls of water.

Whale sharks are not aggressive and will allow divers to approach them.

Filter feeding

Plankton-eating sharks have either spongy filters or rows of fine bars, called rakers, in front of their gills. When the sharks take in mouthfuls of sea water, these rakers or filters help them to capture food by acting like nets, and trapping any plankton in the water.

Small sharks?

Megamouths are the smallest of the plankton eaters, but still reach about 5m (16ft) in length. They live in the open ocean in deep water, and eat plankton, squid and jellyfish.

Amazing mouth

The inside of the upper jaw of a megamouth is luminous and glows in the dark. This may attract prey into its mouth.

Megamouths get their name because of their huge mouths.

Surface sharks

Basking sharks are the second biggest fish in the world. They get their name from their frequent appearances at the surface of the water, where they seem to be enjoying lazing in the sun. In fact, they are feeding, taking water into their huge mouths and filtering it over their rakers.

A basking shark swims with its mouth open to feed on plankton.

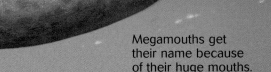
Fact: Scientists think that during winter when there is little food around basking sharks may hibernate, or rest, on the seabed for several months.

Camouflaged sharks

Some types of sharks are very hard to see because they blend in with the reefs and seabeds where they live. This is called camouflage.

Flat shark

Angel sharks are mainly sandy-brown and some have dark blotches over their flat, broad bodies. This means that, when they are resting, they can lie flat against sandy seabeds without being seen.

See how well this Pacific angel shark blends in with the seabed.

A quick bite

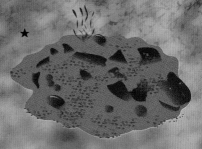

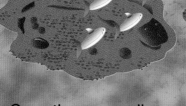

To hunt, angel sharks lie on the seabed and use their pectoral fins to flick sand onto their bodies.

Once they are well covered with sand and are hard to see, they wait for some fish to swim by.

When a fish gets close, the angel shark suddenly attacks, catching its victim in its sharp teeth.

Wobbegongs

Wobbegongs are strange-looking sharks with brightly-patterned skin. They can easily hide among the coral reefs and rocks where they live.

From above, the wobbegong's dark patches look like rocks.

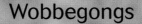

This shark is called an ornate wobbegong because of its brightly-patterned skin.

Seaweed skin

Lobes

This tasselled wobbegong has a fringe of lobes around the front of its head.

Most wobbegongs have pieces of skin, called lobes, hanging down on either side of their heads. These look a little like coral or seaweed.

A deadly surprise

This shows how a wobbegong grabs its prey.

Wobbegongs catch their prey in a similar way to angel sharks. They lie on the seabed waiting to surprise their prey. Then, when a fish comes too close, the wobbegong quickly snatches it.

Fact: The wobbegong was given its strange name by native people of Australia, called Aborigines.

Life on the bottom......................................

Many sharks live near the seabed. These kinds of sharks are usually quite sluggish and like to rest on the bottom. When they hunt, they use the barbels on their snouts to find food.

Nurse sharks

Nurse sharks are often seen in shallow water on rocky reefs, or sandy seabeds which blend in with their brown, flattened bodies.

This nurse shark is swimming over a reef in the Caribbean, an area where many nurse sharks live.

Sleepy sharks

Nurse sharks often take rests. They find a quiet cave or sheltered spot and then pile on top of each other for protection. They rest during the day and hunt at night.

Nurse sharks pile on top of each other during the day.

Protected zebras

Zebra sharks get their name because baby zebra sharks have a striped pattern on their skin. This makes it hard for predators to see young zebra sharks on the tropical reefs where they live. As the sharks grow older, the stripes become dots.

This young zebra shark's skin pattern is clear to see when it is not hidden among rocks and reefs.

Denticles

A barbel

Saw sharks

Saw sharks live on sandy seabeds. Their long snouts have tooth-like denticles on both edges, which make their snouts look like saws.

Saw sharks are about 1.5m (5ft) long. Their snouts take up about a third of their whole length.

Deadly snouts

★

Saw sharks use the long barbels on their snouts to find animals hiding under sand on the seabed.

When a saw shark finds some prey, it uses its snout to dig up the sandy seabed.

If the prey tries to escape, the saw shark attacks it by hitting it with its long, sharp snout.

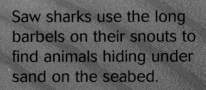

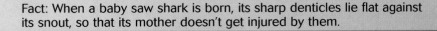

Fact: When a baby saw shark is born, its sharp denticles lie flat against its snout, so that its mother doesn't get injured by them.

33

Reef sharks

Lots of different kinds of plants and animals, including many types of sharks, live on and around reefs. Some of these sharks are actually named reef sharks because of where they live.

Grey reef sharks

Grey reef sharks can be found around the coral reefs of the Indian and Pacific Oceans. They are quite large, active sharks and can grow to 2.5m (8ft) in length.

This grey reef shark is swimming over a coral reef in the Indian Ocean.

Warning signals

If a grey reef shark feels threatened or anxious, it may decide to attack before it is attacked itself. Luckily it gives warning signals first.

When a grey reef shark is troubled by a nearby diver, it starts to arch its back as a warning.

The shark then dips its pectoral fins and thrashes its head from side to side.

When this happens, the diver should calmly swim away or the shark may soon launch an attack.

Blacktips

Blacktip reef sharks often live around coral reefs, but they are also found in areas away from reefs, such as in the middle of the Mediterranean Sea.

Internet links

For links to websites where you can meet sharks and other creatures that live around coral reefs and explore a reef in an online game, go to www.usborne-quicklinks.com

Blacktip reef sharks are easily recognized by the black tips of their fins.

Foot biters

Blacktip reef sharks are 2m (6ft) long, but can move into very shallow water where people may walk or swim. Some people have had their feet bitten by these unexpected attackers.

Reef robbers

Many reef sharks are very curious and will often come close to divers. They have even been known to steal fish caught on the spears of fishermen hunting underwater.

Hammerheads.......

Hammerhead sharks are perhaps the most recognizable fish in the sea. Their wide, flat heads look strange, but enable them to be effective hunters.

Common scallops

Scalloped hammerheads are the most common of the nine types of hammerheads. They get their name from the scallops, or curves, on the front of their heads.

The scallops, or curves, are clearly visible on the head of this scalloped hammerhead.

Great hammers

The great hammerhead shark is the biggest and most fearsome hammerhead. It can reach 6m (18ft) in length and has attacked people.

Great hammerheads are often found near coral reefs or in coastal areas.

Swinging hammers

Hammerheads have eyes at both sides of their heads, which means that they have a very wide field of vision. To see in front of them, they swing their heads from side to side.

A close-up of the eye at one side of a hammerhead's wide head.

The red arrows show the range of vision of a hammerhead shark.

Sensitive heads

Hammerheads are very effective hunters and can easily track down their prey.

The shape of a great hammerhead's head helps it to trap its prey as it attacks.

As hammerheads have wide heads, there is a lot of space on their snouts for the holes, or pores, that detect electric signals given off by other animals. This means they are very good at finding prey.

Great hammerheads use their wide heads to pin stingrays to the seabed. Stingrays have poisonous spines on their tails. But even if hammerheads are stung, they take no notice and just continue their attack.

Internet links

For links to websites where you can meet a shark expert and find out more about hammerhead sharks, go to **www.usborne-quicklinks.com**

Shark schools

Some species of hammerhead sharks often swim around in large groups called schools. Scalloped hammerheads form schools of 200 or more. They swim together during the day but then hunt alone at night.

This is a school of scalloped hammerheads. Nobody is sure why sharks come together in such large numbers.

Cats and hounds

Catsharks and houndsharks are distant relatives, but they have some things in common. They like to eat shellfish and crabs and many of them are well camouflaged.

Swell camouflaged

The swellshark is a patterned catshark, with brown spots all over its yellowish-brown skin. It blends in with the seabed where it lives, and uses this camouflage to help it catch fish and crabs that come too close.

This swellshark is well hidden by the fan coral behind it and the rocks it is resting on.

The balloon shark

When swellsharks feel threatened, they can swell up their bodies so that they look bigger than they really are. This discourages many attackers.

When a swellshark is threatened by another fish or shark it quickly hides among rocks.

It then swallows water and expands its body to make itself look bigger and stronger.

The other shark is less likely to attack and the swellshark is safe inside its hiding place.

Fact: There are at least 90 different species of catsharks – more than any other kind of shark.

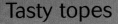

Tasty topes

Soupfin sharks, or topes, are coppery-brown houndsharks, found in coastal waters all around the world. They are widely hunted for their meat, especially for their fins, which are used to make shark fin soup.

Soupfin sharks, or topes, are active swimmers and often make long journeys across oceans.

Gummy sharks

Gummy sharks from Australia get their name from their flat, blunt teeth, and not because they don't have any teeth. They use them to crush the hard shells of lobsters and crabs.

This is a gummy shark crushing the shell of a lobster.

Leopard sharks

Leopard sharks get their name from their brightly-patterned skin. They are harmless, but they are sometimes mistaken for young tiger sharks. Tiger sharks also have patterned skin, but are much more dangerous.

Slow, sluggish leopard sharks can often be seen close to the seabed.

Fast sharks ....

A number of sharks are fast, energetic swimmers, and the fastest sharks are among the quickest swimmers in the sea. Sharks reach their top speeds in short bursts when hunting.

Blue sharks

Blue sharks have long, slender bodies and pointed snouts, which allow them to slip quickly and easily through the water. They are one of the fastest sharks and can reach 60kph (40mph) when chasing after their prey.

Blue sharks travel all over the world, but they prefer cooler water. So, when they are in hot tropical areas, they usually swim down to deeper waters where it is a lot cooler.

Blue sharks swimming in the Pacific Ocean

A blue shark's long, pointed snout juts out a long way over its lower jaw.

Speed feeding

Blue sharks eat many types of prey, including squid, tuna and anchovies. When a hungry blue shark finds a large group of fish, it speeds through the group with its mouth open, devouring as many as it can all at once.

Blue sharks swimming through a group of anchovies to feed.

Powerful makos

Makos are the fastest sharks and they
are also one of the fastest fish. They
can easily match the speeds of fast-
swimming prey, such as marlins and
swordfish. They have powerful tails with
equal-sized lobes, which thrust them
through the water. They can swim at
twice the speed of a top human sprinter.

Makos spend most of
their time in the open
ocean, so swimmers
rarely encounter these
large, powerful sharks.

This is how a mako
hurls its body out
of the water.

Internet links

For links to websites where you can
watch video clips of the fastest-
swimming sharks and see how a
shark compares with other sea
creatures in a race, go to
www.usborne-quicklinks.com

Big jumpers

Makos are such strong sharks that they
can throw themselves right out of the
water. Usually they do this when they are
caught on a fishing line and are fighting
to get free of it. They have sometimes
even jumped into fishing boats.

Deep-water sharks

While many sharks live in fairly shallow water, others spend a lot of their time in the depths of the world's oceans, where the water is very cold and very dark.

Spiny shark

Spiny, or piked, dogfish are one of the most common types of sharks and are found in many parts of the world.

In the winter they live at depths of 800m (2,500ft), but in spring and autumn they prefer shallow water near the coast.

Spiny dogfish have slightly poisonous spikes, or spines, on their dorsal fins, which is how they get their name.

Frilled shark

This is a frilled shark. It is also known as an eel shark because of its long, thin body.

Frilled sharks have six gill slits, each with a frilled, or ridged, band of skin around it. They live as far down as 1,300m (4,000ft) and feed on deep-water fish and squid.

 Internet links

For links to websites where you can search for deep-sea creatures and spot a "sixgill shark", and see photos of other deep-water sharks, go to www.usborne-quicklinks.com

Cookiecutters

Cookiecutters are strange-looking, luminous sharks. They spend the day at depths of 1,000m (3,000ft) and only rise to the surface at night. Although they are only 50cm (20in) long, which is smaller than a cat, they attack large prey such as tuna and dolphins.

Cookiecutters are also called cigar sharks. This is because of their size, shape and brown skin.

Dolphins are a popular target of hungry cookiecutters.

Suck and munch

Cookiecutters have soft, padded lips. They attack other animals by sucking an area of flesh into their mouths and taking small round bites.

Deep sea diver

Portuguese sharks have been found nearly 3,700m (over two miles) beneath the sea's surface. They live so deep down that experts don't know much about them.

This diagram shows where Portuguese sharks live in relation to some other sharks.

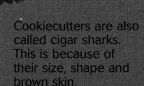

Basking sharks live close to the surface.

Frilled sharks live quite deep down at 1,300m (4,000ft).

Portuguese sharks live at depths of 3,700m (12,000ft).

Shark relatives

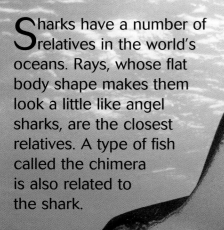

Sharks have a number of relatives in the world's oceans. Rays, whose flat body shape makes them look a little like angel sharks, are the closest relatives. A type of fish called the chimera is also related to the shark.

How rays swim

Rays swim differently from sharks. Some flap their pectoral fins up and down like wings. Others swim along by rippling the edges of their pectoral fins, from front to back.

This eagle ray moves by flapping its pectoral fins up and down.

Are rays like sharks?

Like sharks, rays have flexible skeletons, can sense electric signals given off by other animals and use gills to breathe.

But unlike sharks, many rays have poisonous spines on their tails, which they use to defend themselves against large fish.

Poisonous spine

This southern stingray is resting on the sandy seabed of the Atlantic Ocean.

Fact: There are about six hundred different types of rays, found all over the world, both in the oceans and in fresh water.

Electric rays

Some rays can produce electric shocks to surprise and stun both predators and prey. Divers who have accidentally touched an electric ray hiding on the seabed have received bad shocks.

Gigantic mantas

The most impressive-looking ray is the huge manta ray. It is nearly 7m (23ft) wide, which is wider than four cars next to each other. Like the biggest sharks, it is also a harmless plankton eater.

Here you can see two huge lobes in front of this manta ray's eyes. It uses these to guide plankton into its mouth.

Lobe

An elephantfish swimming in deep water off the coast of New Zealand

Underwater elephants

Chimeras are distant relatives of sharks and mostly live in deep water. They too use electric signals to find prey, and have flexible skeletons. One strange-looking chimera is the elephantfish, which has a snout shaped like an elephant's trunk.

On the move

Sometimes sharks travel to new places to look for food, to mate, to give birth or simply to find warmer waters. This is called migrating.

This blue shark is swimming along its regular route across the North Atlantic Ocean accompanied by a large school of jack mackerel.

Long and short migrations

Some sharks travel hundreds of miles once or twice a year. But not all migrations are over such long distances.

A number of sharks make daily trips from deep water to nearer the surface, where more fish and other prey live.

Transatlantic blues

Blue sharks in the North Atlantic regularly make a loop-shaped journey across the ocean. They are following water currents, which are moving bands of warm or cold water.

The blue arrows show the route taken by blue sharks in the North Atlantic.

Fact: Some blue sharks swim more than 4,000 km (2,500 miles) in a year.

Wandering whale sharks

Every March or April, large numbers of whale sharks make a special journey to a place called Ningaloo Reef, off the west coast of Australia. They do this because, at this time, there are huge quantities of plankton there for the whale sharks to eat.

A whale shark swimming above Ningaloo Reef

Busy pygmies

Every day, after sunset, pygmy sharks leave the deep water where they live, and swim up to the surface to feed. They then return to the deep before morning.

Pygmy sharks are small – not more than 26cm (10in) in length. So their daily journey of 3km (2 miles) is a long one for them.

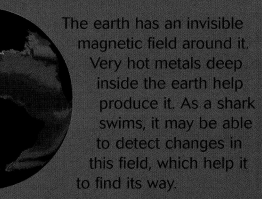

Some pygmy sharks are small enough to fit into a person's hand.

On the right track

Nobody is sure how sharks find their way through the world's oceans. They may be guided by changes in water temperature.

This globe shows how sea temperatures vary. Red areas show warm water, and blue areas show cold water.

The earth has an invisible magnetic field around it. Very hot metals deep inside the earth help produce it. As a shark swims, it may be able to detect changes in this field, which help it to find its way.

Shark attacks.......................................

Shark attacks are sometimes deadly, but they are also very rare. Between five and ten people worldwide are killed by sharks each year. Many more people die by drowning than by shark attack.

Accidental attacks

Most shark attacks happen by accident because sharks confuse people in the sea for prey like seals. Once they have attacked, they usually realize their mistake and swim off.

Look out for signs on beaches warning about the presence of sharks in the sea.

MUNICIPALITY OF ROCKDALE

DANGER

SHARKS IN BOTANY BAY

From below, the shape of a surfboard and the surfer's legs looks similar to a seal or turtle's body.

Where do sharks attack?

Sharks live all over the world but many attacks happen in the seas around North America (particularly in Florida and Hawaii), Australia and South Africa.

In these places the warm water attracts people, and brings them into possible contact with sharks.

North America Europe Asia Africa South America Australasia

■ The red areas on this map indicate where most shark attacks take place.

Fact: Many shark attacks occur less than 30m (100ft) from the shore.

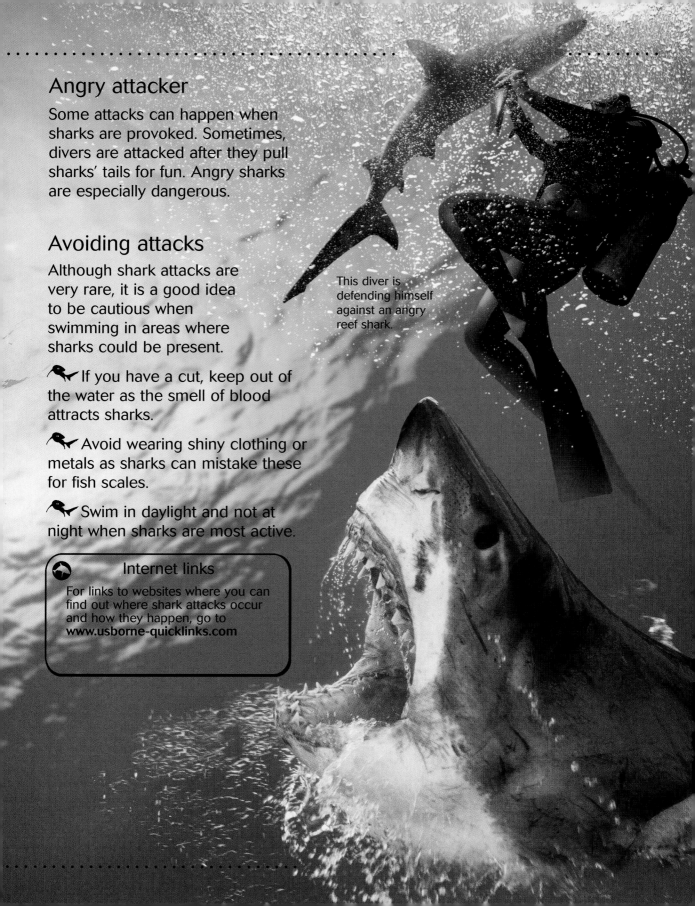

Angry attacker

Some attacks can happen when sharks are provoked. Sometimes, divers are attacked after they pull sharks' tails for fun. Angry sharks are especially dangerous.

Avoiding attacks

Although shark attacks are very rare, it is a good idea to be cautious when swimming in areas where sharks could be present.

If you have a cut, keep out of the water as the smell of blood attracts sharks.

Avoid wearing shiny clothing or metals as sharks can mistake these for fish scales.

Swim in daylight and not at night when sharks are most active.

This diver is defending himself against an angry reef shark.

Internet links

For links to websites where you can find out where shark attacks occur and how they happen, go to **www.usborne-quicklinks.com**

Sharks in danger

Humans may fear sharks, but sharks also have every reason to fear humans. People kill them for sport, food, or sometimes just by mistake.

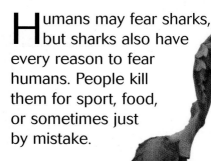

Hunted hunters

Although sharks rarely attack people, they are thought of as dangerous. So, catching them is a tough challenge for hunters, who often keep shark jaws as souvenirs or sell them to tourists.

This hunter proudly displays two sets of shark jaws.

Unfair finning

Soup made from shark fins is a popular dish in some parts of the world. Sometimes when sharks are caught, fishermen cruelly cut off their fins and throw the sharks back into the sea. Without their fins, sharks are unable to swim. They can't get enough oxygen or hunt for food and so they eventually die.

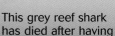

This grey reef shark has died after having its fins cut off.

Killer nets

Huge nets laid to catch fish like tuna kill millions of sharks each year as well. In some countries, safety nets are placed close to beaches to protect people from dangerous sharks. Unfortunately, these nets trap and kill many harmless sharks too.

Once a shark becomes entangled in a fishing net, it has little chance of escape and may die.

Internet links

For links to websites where you can see a counter showing how many sharks are killed every second, and find out more about sharks in danger, go to www.usborne-quicklinks.com

Endangered sharks

Every year, as many as 100 million sharks are killed. As a result, some types of sharks are in danger of completely dying out. For example, over five million blue sharks are caught each year, and so their numbers have fallen sharply.

Blue sharks are less common than they were, because large numbers of them have been hunted and killed. Many are caught for their fins.

Studying sharks

For many years, people knew very little about sharks. But advances in science and technology mean that we now have a much better idea of what sharks are like and how they live.

Tagging

One way of studying sharks is to tag them. First, a shark is caught, then it is measured and weighed, and details about where and when it was found are written on a tag. The tag is stuck into one of its fins. The shark is then set free. If it is later recaptured, scientists can estimate its age, how much it has grown and how far it tends to travel.

Sonic sharks

Some tags are electronic. They give off high-pitched sound signals which can be detected by a receiver on board a boat following a shark. This enables scientists to track the exact movements of the shark.

Here, a scientist is tagging a tiger shark underwater, without catching it first.

Once a shark swims down into deeper water, or gets a long way ahead of the boat, tag signals become too weak to follow.

Fact: In 1991, off the Australian coast, a soupfin shark was recaptured that had been tagged over forty years before.

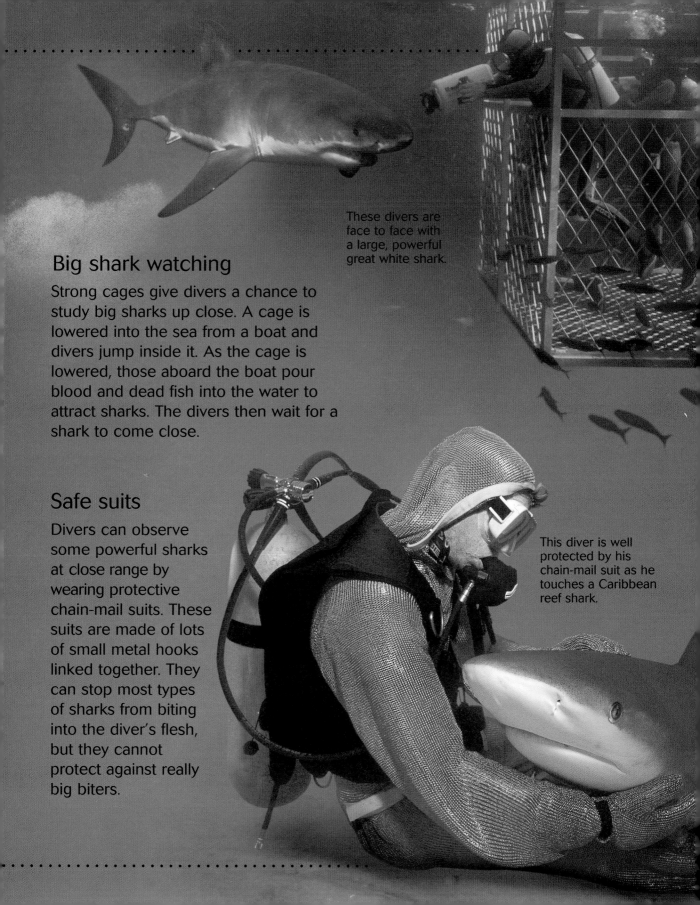

Big shark watching

Strong cages give divers a chance to study big sharks up close. A cage is lowered into the sea from a boat and divers jump inside it. As the cage is lowered, those aboard the boat pour blood and dead fish into the water to attract sharks. The divers then wait for a shark to come close.

These divers are face to face with a large, powerful great white shark.

Safe suits

Divers can observe some powerful sharks at close range by wearing protective chain-mail suits. These suits are made of lots of small metal hooks linked together. They can stop most types of sharks from biting into the diver's flesh, but they cannot protect against really big biters.

This diver is well protected by his chain-mail suit as he touches a Caribbean reef shark.

Sharks in a changing world

Sharks face many dangers in the modern world, but the threat from pollution is one of the worst.

Equipment on this barge is being used to burn oil that has spilled into the sea and is threatening nearby wildlife.

Long-term threats

Sharks are used to adapting to sudden short-term changes to their habitats (where they live) due to stormy seas or bad weather. But human activities such as fishing and shipping, and waste from industry, are causing long-term damage to their habitats.

Pollution

Pollution means any waste that builds up quicker than it can be broken down. It includes chemicals from industry, and sewage and oil leaks from ships. The huge amount of water in the world's oceans can absorb a lot of waste, but not all of it.

Large amounts of pollution can build up in a shark's body when it feeds on animals that have been poisoned.

These sharks are lying dead in polluted water.

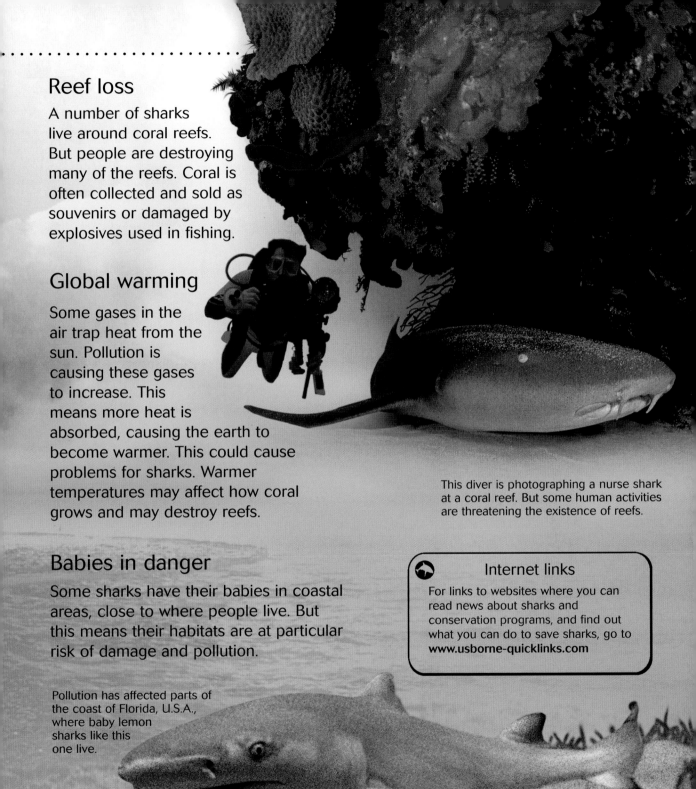

Reef loss

A number of sharks live around coral reefs. But people are destroying many of the reefs. Coral is often collected and sold as souvenirs or damaged by explosives used in fishing.

Global warming

Some gases in the air trap heat from the sun. Pollution is causing these gases to increase. This means more heat is absorbed, causing the earth to become warmer. This could cause problems for sharks. Warmer temperatures may affect how coral grows and may destroy reefs.

This diver is photographing a nurse shark at a coral reef. But some human activities are threatening the existence of reefs.

Babies in danger

Some sharks have their babies in coastal areas, close to where people live. But this means their habitats are at particular risk of damage and pollution.

Internet links

For links to websites where you can read news about sharks and conservation programs, and find out what you can do to save sharks, go to **www.usborne-quicklinks.com**

Pollution has affected parts of the coast of Florida, U.S.A., where baby lemon sharks like this one live.

Shark bites

Sharks are fascinating animals and a lot is still not known about their lives and habits. Here are some bite-sized chunks of information about these intriguing creatures.

A grey reef shark swimming in shallow water

Pilot fish often swim alongside sharks. These small, striped fish look as if they are guiding their larger companions. But, in fact, they are staying close to them for protection from predators.

About two-thirds of shark attacks on humans have taken place in water less than 2m (6ft) deep.

These striped pilot fish are being protected by the oceanic whitetip swimming behind them.

Until the 19th century, in some islands in the Pacific Ocean, sharks were considered to be gods and human sacrifices were offered up to them.

Spiny dogfish pups spend almost two years inside their mothers before they are ready to be born.

Although there are about four hundred different types of sharks, fewer than 20% of them are larger than humans.

A spiny dogfish

This pelagic thresher shark has a tail 1.5m (5ft) long.

Men are much more likely to be attacked by sharks than women are. About 90% of shark attacks have happened to men. As almost equal numbers of men and women spend time in the sea, nobody is really sure why sharks seem to prefer to attack men.

Thresher sharks have long tails which are equal in length to the rest of their bodies. When flicked from side-to-side, the tail can be a powerful weapon.

Shark attacks are so rare that people are far more likely to be killed by a bolt of lightning or die from a bee sting than be eaten by a shark.

Sharks almost never get cancer. Scientific research exploring the reasons for this may one day help to provide a cure for this serious disease.

Fish called remoras use suction pads on their heads to attach themselves to a shark's body. They can then get a ride as the shark swims along. Remoras also like to eat any food scraps left by sharks.

This remora is getting a ride on a nurse shark.

Shark skin can be used to make a whole range of things. In the past, it was used to cover sword handles and boxes, but these days handbags, shoes and wallets are sometimes made from it.

Record breakers

As there are so many different types of sharks, there is a whole range of interesting shark records to explore — from the biggest to the smallest and the most common to the rarest.

The largest shark is the whale shark, which reaches 14m (46ft) in length. It is also the largest fish in the sea.

A diver looks very small alongside the biggest fish in the sea.

Whale sharks give birth to the greatest number of pups. They can produce several hundred in one litter.

One of the rarest sharks is the mysterious megamouth. Since the first one was discovered in 1976, only 14 have ever been seen.

The fastest shark is the mako, which may reach speeds of up to 100kph (60mph) in short bursts. Other fast swimmers include the blue shark and the porbeagle.

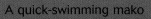

A quick-swimming mako

A rarely seen megamouth

Internet links

For links to websites with shark videos and fascinating facts, go to www.usborne-quicklinks.com

Website 1 Watch video clips of the largest shark in the world, the whale shark.

Website 2 Meet the second largest fish in the world, the basking shark.

Website 3 Watch an animation of a megalodon, a prehistoric shark, and see what scientists think it looked like.

Great whites are large,
powerful and dangerous.

🦈 The shark that lives the longest
is the spiny, or piked, dogfish. These
sharks usually live to about seventy
years of age, but some may live
until they are a hundred years old.

🦈 The spiny, or piked, dogfish is
the most common shark. But
it is also very widely hunted
and its numbers have
dropped in recent years.

🦈 The smallest sharks
are the spined pygmy shark
and the dwarf dogfish. Both
of these are only about
16-22cm (6-9in) long.

🦈 Great whites are thought
to be the most dangerous sharks
of all. During the 1990s at least
ten people were killed by them.

🦈 Sleeper sharks live in the coldest
waters. The Greenland sleeper shark is
found in deep water near the North Pole.
Several other sharks, such as the
porbeagle, also live in cold surroundings.

🦈 A huge prehistoric shark called
the megalodon may have been the
biggest shark ever.
It reached about
15m (50ft) in
length. One of
its teeth was
almost as big as
a man's hand.

A megalodon's tooth

Glossary

On these pages are some of the words and phrases you may come across when reading about sharks. Any word that appears in *italic* type is defined elsewhere in the glossary.

ampullae of Lorenzini Black dots on a shark's head that enable it to detect electric signals sent out by other animals.

anal fin A single fin close to a shark's tail.

barbel A fleshy strip of skin near a shark's mouth, which it uses to feel for food.

camouflage Body markings which help an animal to blend in with its background.

cartilage A hard, bendy material. Shark skeletons are made of it.

conservation Protecting and preserving our natural surroundings, and the plants and animals living in them.

coral The skeletons of tiny animals known as coral polyps.

coral reef A ridge in the sea made up of *coral*.

current A flow of water, running steadily through the oceans.

denticle A small thorn-like hook on a shark's skin. It helps protect a shark from injury.

dorsal fin A large fin on a shark's back which helps it to stay balanced while swimming.

electrosensory system A way sharks have of finding other animals by detecting the electric signals they send out.

endangered Under threat. Endangered *species* are groups of animals or plants which are in serious danger of dying out.

environment The natural surroundings in which plants and animals live.

extinction The gradual process where a *species* of plants or animals completely dies out.

feeding frenzy The way a group of sharks can become over-excited while feeding, attacking anything in their path, including each other.

filter-feeding Eating by straining food, such as *plankton*, out of the water – often using *gill rakers*.

gill A part of the body which sharks and fish use to absorb oxygen from sea water.

gill raker A stiff comb-like bar in the *gills*, which some *filter-feeding* sharks use to catch *plankton* floating in the water.

gill slit An opening behind a shark's eyes that contains a *gill*. Most sharks have five, but some have six or seven.

global warming Gradual increase in world temperatures, partly caused by *pollution*.

habitat The place where a group of animals or plants lives.

hibernation A sleep-like resting period that some animals regularly go into for several months during winter.

lateral line A pair of tubes stretching along the entire length of a shark's body, just under its skin. With them, a shark can detect tiny movements of its prey.

marine Something found in, or relating to, the sea.

mate To come together to breed and as a result produce young.

migration The process of moving from one *habitat* to another made by some animals at certain times of the year.

nictitating eyelids Thin protective layers of skin which move across to cover the eyes of some types of sharks when they attack prey.

pectoral fins The fins on either side of a shark's body found just behind its *gill slits*.

pelvic fins The small fins on either side of a shark's body just in front of the *anal fin*.

plankton Very tiny animals or plants that float in the sea.

polar Something relating to the cold areas around the North and South Poles.

pollution Waste which builds up and poisons the *environment*, often killing plants and animals.

predator An animal that hunts and kills other animals for food.

prey An animal that is hunted for food by other animals, or *predators*.

pup A young shark.

reef A ridge of rock, sand or coral. The top is usually very close to the surface of the sea.

school A group of fish, or other sea animals, swimming together.

species (plural: species) A type of plant or animal.

spiracle A small round opening behind a shark's eye, which allows it to breathe in oxygen without opening its mouth.

tag To attach a label or marker to a shark's skin.

tapetum (plural: tapeta) A reflective layer at the back of a shark's eye, which helps the shark to see better in the dark.

temperate Mild. Neither very hot, nor very cold.

tropical Something relating to the hot and humid areas of the tropics.

yolk A liquid inside eggs that provides food and nutrients for a developing animal.

yolk sac A thin skin, or sac, surrounding the *yolk* of an egg.

Internet links

Throughout this book we have recommended websites where you can find out more about sharks. To visit the sites, go to the **Usborne Quicklinks Website** where you will find links to all the sites.

1. Go to **www.usborne-quicklinks.com**
2. Type the keywords for this book: **discovery sharks**
3. Type the page number of the link you want to visit.
4. Click on the link to go to the recommended site.

Here are some of the things you can do on the websites recommended in this book:
- Watch exciting video clips of sharks.
- Explore a coral reef and find sharks that live there.
- Play a survival game as a hungry tiger shark.
- Watch an animation of a prehistoric shark.

Site availability

The links in Usborne Quicklinks are regularly reviewed and updated, but occasionally you may get a message that a site is unavailable. This might be temporary, so try again later, or even the next day. Websites do occasionally close down and when this happens, we will replace them with new links in Usborne Quicklinks. Sometimes we add extra links too, if we think they are useful. So when you visit Usborne Quicklinks, the links may be slightly different from those described in your book.

Downloadable pictures

Pictures marked with a ★ in this book can be downloaded from the Usborne Quicklinks Website. These pictures are for personal use only and must not be used for commercial purposes.

> **COMPUTER NOT ESSENTIAL**
> If you don't have access to the internet, don't worry. This book is a fun and informative introduction to sharks on its own.

Safety on the internet

Ask your parent's or guardian's permission before you connect to the internet and make sure you follow these simple rules:

- Never give out information about yourself, such as your real name, address, phone number or the name of your school.
- If a site asks you to log in or register by typing your name or email address, ask permission from an adult first.

What you need

To visit the websites you need a computer with an internet connection and a web browser (the software that lets you look at information from the internet). Some sites need extra programs (plug-ins) to play sound or show videos or animations.

If you go to a site and do not have the necessary plug-in, a message will come up on the screen. There is usually a link to click on to download the plug-in. For more information about plug-ins, go to Usborne Quicklinks and click on "Net Help".

Notes for parents and guardians

The websites described in this book are regularly reviewed, but the content of a website may change at any time and Usborne Publishing is not responsible for the content on any website other than its own.

We recommend that children are supervised while on the internet, that they do not use internet chat rooms, and that you use internet filtering software to block unsuitable material. Please ensure that your children read and follow the safety guidelines printed above. For more information, see the Net Help area on the Usborne Quicklinks Website.

Index ....

Acknowledgements....................................

Every effort has been made to trace the copyright holders of the material in this book. If any rights have been omitted, the publishers offer to rectify this in any subsequent editions following notification. The publishers are grateful to the following organizations and individuals for their permission to reproduce material (t=top, m=middle, b=bottom, l=left, r=right):

Cover © Tim Davis/Corbis; © Stockbyte; **p1** Richard Herrmann/Innerspace Visions; **p2** (m) Steve Drogin/Innerspace Visions; **p3** (br) Walt Stearns/Innerspace Visions; **p4** (m) Franco Banfi/Innerspace Visions, (bl) Bob Cranston/Innerspace Visions, (br) Doug Perrine/Innerspace Visions; **p5** (tr) Tom Campbell/Innerspace Visions, (br) Digital Vision ©; **p6-7** (m) Doug Perrine/ Innerspace Visions; **p8** (m) James D. Watt/Innerspace Visions; **p9** (t) Doug Perrine/Innerspace Visions, (br) Jeffrey Jaskolski/ Innerspace Visions; **p10** (m) James Watt/Innerspace Visions, (bl) Doug Perrine/Innerspace Visions; **p11** (br) Bill Harrigan/ Innerspace Visions; **p12** (bl) Marty Snyderman/Innerspace Visions, (tr) Jeff Rotman/Innerspace Visions; **p13** (t) David Fleetham/ Innerspace Visions, (br) Norbert Wu/Innerspace Visions; **p14** (m) Jeff Rotman/Innerspace Visions; **p15** (br) Doug Perrine/ Innerspace Visions; **p16** (tl) Bob Cranston/Innerspace Visions, (bl) David Fleetham/Innerspace Visions; **p17** (tl) Doug Perrine/ Innerspace Visions, (tr) Mark Conlin/Innerspace Visions, (br) Ardea/Ron and Valerie Taylor; **p18** (r) James D. Watt/Innerspace Visions; **p19** (m) Steve Drogin/Innerspace Visions; **p20** (m) Michel Jozon/Innerspace Visions; **p21** (tr) Jeff Rotman/Innerspace Visions, (b) Doug Perrine/Innerspace Visions; **p22** (t) © AFP/Corbis, (bl) Mark Conlin/Innerspace Visions; **p23** (tr) Nigel Marsh/ Innerspace Visions, (b) Mark Conlin/Innerspace Visions; **p24** (l) James D. Watt/Innerspace Visions; **p24-25** (m) Kelvin Aitken/ Still Pictures; **p26** (m) Ben Cropp Productions/Innerspace Visions; **p27** (t) Doug Perrine/Innerspace Visions, (b) Doug Perrine/ Innerspace Visions; **p28** (b) Mark Strickland/Innerspace Visions; **p29** (tr) Tom Haight/Innerspace Visions, (b) Jeff Rotman/BBC Natural History Unit Picture Library; **p30** (t) James D. Watt/Innerspace Visions; **p31** (t) David B. Fleetham/Innerspace Visions, (bl) Howard Hall/Innerspace Visions; **p32** (m) Doug Perrine/Innerspace Visions; **p33** (tr) Nicholas Penn/Planet Earth Pictures, (m) Marty Snyderman/Innerspace Visions; **p34** (m) Kurt Amsler/Innerspace Visions, (b) Doug Perrine/Innerspace Visions; **p35** (t) David B. Fleetham/Innerspace Visions, (b) Telegraph Colour Library/Gary Bell; **p36** (t) Doug Perrine/Innerspace Visions, (bl) Gary Adkinson/Innerspace Visions, (bm) Jeff Rotman/Innerspace Visions; **p37** (b) Marty Snyderman/Innerspace Visions; **p38** (tr) Mark Conlin/Innerspace Visions; **p39** (t) Doug Perrine/Innerspace Visions, (br) ©Patrice Ceisel/Stock/Boston; **p40** (l) Michael Nolan/Innerspace Visions, (bl) Richard Herrmann/Innerspace Visions; **p41** (m) Howard Hall/Innerspace Visions; **p42** (tr) Chris Huss/Innerspace Visions, (m) Rudie Kuiter/Innerspace Visions; **p43** (tr) Norbert Wu/Innerspace Visions; **p44** (tl) Ardea/Ron and Valerie Taylor, (b) Georgette Douwma/Planet Earth Pictures; **p45** (m) D. D. Seifert/Planet Earth Pictures, (b) NHPA/ANT; **p46** (m) Richard Herrmann/Innerspace Visions; **p47** (t) James D. Watt/Innerspace Visions, (mr) Gwen Lowe/Innerspace Visions, (bm) Los Alamos National Laboratory/Science Photo Library; **p48** (t) Doug Perrine/Innerspace Visions, (ml) Bob Cranston/Innerspace Visions; **p49** (tr) ©Jeffery L. Rotman/Corbis, (b) Amos Nachoum/Innerspace Visions; **p50** (t) ©Jeffery L. Rotman/Corbis, (b) Mark Strickland/Innerspace Visions; **p51** (t) ©Tony Arruza/Corbis, (b) Richard Herrmann/Innerspace Visions; **p52** (m) Doug Perrine/Innerspace Visions; **p53** (t) ©Jeffery L. Rotman/Corbis, (b) Bill Harrigan/Innerspace Visions; **p54** (t) ©Stephen Frink/ Corbis, (br) Ardea/Ian Beames; **p55** (t) ©Lowell Georgia/Corbis, (b) Doug Perrine/Innerspace Visions; **p56** (tr) ©Jonathan Blair/ Corbis, (b) Chris Huss/Innerspace Visions; **p56-57** (m) David B. Fleetham/Innerspace Visions; **p57** (t) Ferrari/Watt/Innerspace Visions, (br) ©Jeffery L. Rotman/Corbis; **p58** (t) David B. Fleetham/Innerspace Visions, (mr) David Hall/Innerspace Visions, (bl) Bruce Rasner/Innerspace Visions; **p59** (t) David Fleetham/Innerspace Visions, (bm) Bob Cranston/Innerspace Visions.

Series editor: Gill Doherty; Managing editor: Jane Chisholm; Managing designer: Mary Cartwright
Photographic manipulation: John Russell; Cover design: Zoe Wray

Usborne Publishing has made every effort to ensure that material on the Web sites listed in this book is suitable for its intended purpose. However, we do not accept responsibility, and are not responsible, for any Web site other than our own. Nor will we be liable for any exposure to harmful, offensive, or inaccurate material which may appear on the Web. We recommend that children are supervised when using the Internet.

Usborne cannot guarantee that Web sites listed in this book are permanent, or that the addresses given will remain accurate, or that the information on those sites will remain as described. We will endeavour to provide up-to-date lists of addresses in the Quicklinks area of the Usborne Web site at **www.usborne.com**

Usborne Publishing will have no liability for any damage or loss caused by viruses that may be downloaded as a result of browsing the sites we recommend.

• •